I0821600

Smithsonian LITTLE EXPLORER

THE LINCOLN MEMORIAL

All About the American Symbol

by Jessica Gunderson

PEBBLE
a capstone imprint

Pebble Explore is published by Pebble, an imprint of Capstone.
1710 Roe Crest Drive
North Mankato, Minnesota 56003
www.capstonepub.com

Library of Congress Cataloging-in-Publication Data is available on the Library of Congress website.
ISBN 978-1-9771-2589-7 (library binding)
ISBN 978-1-9771-2609-2 (eBook PDF)
Summary: So much more than a structure honoring the life and work of one man, President Abraham Lincoln, the Lincoln Memorial has become an enduring American symbol of strength and unity. Young report writers will learn why and how the memorial was built and what its many parts mean.

Image Credits
Alamy: National Geographic Image Collection, 15; Library of Congress: 7, 8, 9, 11, 12, 13, 16, 24, 25, 27, Photographs in the Carol M. Highsmith Archive, 1, 5, The Alfred Whital Stern Collection of Lincolniana, 10; Newscom: Everett Collection, 17, World History Archive, 26; Shutterstock: Bill Perry, 18, Kamira, 19, ket-le (banner), back cover and throughout, Lissandra Melo, 29, Lucky-photographer, 20, MGS, 4, Norbert Rehm, cover, Rorbert Rehm, 23, V_E, 21

Editorial Credits
Editor: Jill Kalz; Designer: Juliette Peters; Media Researcher: Svetlana Zhurkin; Production Specialist: Laura Manthe

Our very special thanks to Kealy Gordon, Product Development Manager; Paige Towler; and the following at Smithsonian Enterprises: Jill Corcoran, Director, Licensed Publishing; Brigid Ferraro, Vice President, Consumer and Education Products; and Carol LeBlanc, President, Smithsonian Enterprises.

Printed in the United States of America.
PA117

Table of Contents

Words in **bold** are in the glossary.

Introduction

The United States of America has many **symbols**. Our flag is one of them. So is the bald eagle. They are objects that stand for our country. The Lincoln **Memorial** is also one of those symbols.

The Lincoln Memorial is a large **monument** in Washington, D.C. Inside, there is a statue of Abraham Lincoln. He was one of our most important presidents. The monument is a symbol of freedom and **equality**.

A Great President

Abraham Lincoln was the 16th president of the United States. He served from 1861 to 1865, during the **Civil War**.

The Civil War began after the southern states broke away from the rest of the nation. Much of the south supported the **enslavement** of black people. The north, including the president, did not.

Lincoln knew that both sides needed each other to be a strong nation. He fought to bring all the states back together as one country.

President Abraham Lincoln (center) and members of the Northern Army in 1862

Lincoln was against enslavement. He signed a **document** called the Emancipation Proclamation in 1863. It helped to free enslaved people in the southern states.

Some people didn't like what President Lincoln had done. They thought he was trying to destroy the south. They said their large farms would fail without enslaved workers. In 1865, a man named John Wilkes Booth shot and killed Lincoln.

President Abraham Lincoln (1809–1865)

Honoring Lincoln

In 1867, a group called the Lincoln Monument Association was formed. It wanted to honor President Lincoln with a memorial. The group asked fellow Americans and the government for money to help build it.

People who gave money to the Lincoln Memorial project got a receipt like this in return.

President Howard Taft (1909–1913; far left) supported the Lincoln Memorial project from the start.

How could the nation honor Lincoln? Some people wanted to build a road and name it after him. Others wanted a park. After many years, a monument was chosen. It would be built in Washington, D.C.

Making Plans

Henry Bacon designed the monument. His plans showed three **chambers**. Artist Jules Guerin would paint **murals** inside the two side chambers. The middle chamber would hold a statue of Lincoln.

Henry Bacon

Daniel Chester French designed the statue. He studied paintings and photos of Lincoln. He planned to make a clay model first. Then he would give it to the stonecutters, the Piccirilli Brothers. They would use it to carve a larger statue.

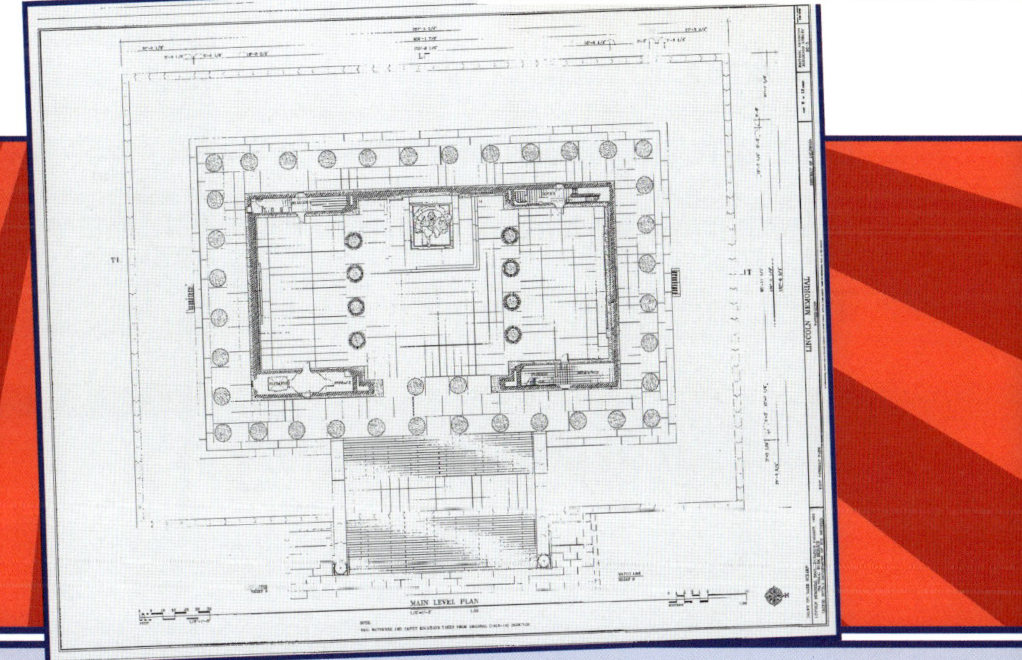

A drawing of the entire Lincoln Memorial, as seen from above

A Grand Spot

Plans for the monument were done. But where should it be built? The best choice seemed to be on the east side of the Potomac River.

The monument would face the U.S. Capitol building. It would also be right across from the Washington Monument. That memorial honors the first U.S. president, George Washington.

Washington, D.C., in 1918

Time to Build

Work began on February 12, 1914. Lincoln was born on that date in 1809.

Daniel Chester French and some of his art, including a model of Lincoln (far left)

Daniel Chester French worked on the statue. He made two models. The second one was slightly larger than the first. It stood 10 feet (3 meters) tall. French put it inside the monument to see how it looked. It was too small! So, French went bigger. The final statue would be 19 feet (5.8 m) tall.

The Lincoln Memorial

The Lincoln Memorial was finished in 1922. It had large steps, three chambers, and 36 stone columns. There was one column for each state when Lincoln was president.

Lincoln's work had brought the states back together after the Civil War. So, Bacon used materials from across the country. He used stone from Alabama, Colorado, Indiana, Massachusetts, and Tennessee.

Two murals were painted. One of them showed an angel setting enslaved people free. The words of the Gettysburg Address were carved below. In that famous speech, Lincoln talked about freedom and equality.

The Lincoln statue, with the south chamber mural and Gettysburg Address to the left

Lincoln's Gettysburg Address

The other mural showed an angel holding the hands of two people. The people stood for the northern and southern states. Below the mural were the words of a speech Lincoln gave just before the Civil War ended.

Lincoln's statue was placed inside the middle chamber. It was carved out of white marble. Marble is a hard, long-lasting stone.

Lincoln's head was slightly bowed. It showed him as a deep thinker. His left hand was in a fist. This showed his power as president. His right hand was open to show his caring side.

Grand Opening

May 30, 1922, was a big day. Thousands of people came to the Lincoln Memorial. They were there for its **dedication**.

Robert Moton gave the main speech. He was the president of the Tuskegee Institute, a college for black Americans. Moton talked about Lincoln helping to free enslaved people. He spoke about equal rights for all Americans.

Some things had gotten better for black Americans since the Civil War. But there was still so much work to do.

To Be Equal

The Lincoln Memorial became a symbol for many black Americans. It stood for freedom and equality.

In 1939, black singer Marian Anderson was told she couldn't sing at a famous concert hall. It was a "whites-only" stage. First Lady Eleanor Roosevelt asked her to sing at the Lincoln Memorial instead. There, Anderson sang to 75,000 people.

Marian Anderson

Martin Luther King Jr. spoke at the monument in 1963. He was a **civil rights** leader. More than 250,000 people listened to his “I Have a Dream” speech.

A Lasting Message

Abraham Lincoln was a strong and caring leader. He fought hard to keep the United States together and to end the Civil War. He believed all people should be free and equal.

Today, our country is still working to finish what Lincoln started. The Lincoln Memorial reminds us of his bravery. The monument is one of our greatest treasures.

Glossary

chamber (CHAYM-bur)—a large room

civil rights (SI-vil RYTS)—freedoms that every person should have

Civil War (SIV-uhl WOR)—(1861–1865) the battle between states in the North and South that led to the freeing of enslaved people in the United States

dedication (de-duh-KAY-shuhn)—an event to mark the opening of something

document (DAHK-yuh-muhnt)—a piece of paper that contains important information

enslavement (en-SLAYV-muhnt)—the taking away of all freedoms and being forced to work for no pay

equality (i-KWAH-luh-tee)—having the same rights or place in society

memorial (muh-MOR-ih-uhl)—something that is built or done to honor an event or person

monument (MON-yoo-muhnt)—a statue or building meant to remind people of an event or person

mural (MYUR-uhl)—a painting that is done on a wall

symbol (SIM-buhl)—a design or an object that stands for something else

Read More

Chang, Kirsten. *The Lincoln Memorial*. Minneapolis: Bellwether Media, Inc., 2019.

Linde, Barbara M. *The Lincoln Memorial*. New York: Gareth Stevens Publishing, 2019.

Murray, Julie. *Lincoln Memorial*. Minneapolis: Abdo Kids, 2017.

Internet Sites

Biography: President Abraham Lincoln
https://www.ducksters.com/biography/uspresidents/abrahamlincoln.php

Lincoln Memorial Facts for Kids
https://kids.kiddle.co/Lincoln_Memorial

National Park Service: Lincoln Memorial
https://www.nps.gov/linc/index.htm

Index